We hope this book has been informative and helpful on your journey to understanding and celebrating older adults. Thank you for your interest and support!

Title: Heritage and Culture-Discovering the Heart and Soul of the Capitals

Subtitle: The Architectural Wonders of Each Capital

Series: Cosmopolitan Chronicles: Tales of the World's Great Cities

By Kelli Tempest

"The world is a book, and those who do not travel read only one page."
Saint Augustine

"A city is not gauged by its length and width, but by the broadness of its vision and the height of its dreams."
Herb Caen

"The purpose of life is to live it, to taste experience to the utmost, to reach out eagerly and without fear for newer and richer experience."
Eleanor Roosevelt

"The only way to do great work is to love what you do."
Steve Jobs

"Travel makes one modest. You see what a tiny place you occupy in the world."
Gustave Flaubert

"Cities were always like people, showing their varying personalities to the traveler. Depending on the city and on the traveler, there might begin a mutual love, or dislike, friendship, or enmity."

Roman Payne

"The best way to predict the future is to create it."
Abraham Lincoln

"The world is a beautiful book, but of little use to him who cannot read it."
Carlo Goldon

"In every walk with nature, one receives far more than he seeks."
John Muir

Table of Contents

Introduction

The importance of history and culture in understanding a city's identity

When we travel to a new city, we often seek out the landmarks, museums, and cultural events that define its character. But have you ever stopped to consider why these things matter? The answer lies in the fact that history and culture are the building blocks of a city's identity.

Every city has a unique story to tell, shaped by the people who lived and worked there, the events that took place, and the cultural traditions that developed over time. By understanding this story, we gain a deeper appreciation for the city's past and present, and we are better equipped to navigate its streets, neighborhoods, and social dynamics.

The role of architecture, art, music, literature, food, and festivals in shaping a city's culture

Architecture, art, music, literature, food, and festivals are all part of a city's cultural heritage. They reflect the values, beliefs, and aspirations of the people who created them, and they provide a window into the city's history and identity.

For example, a city's architecture can reveal its social and economic history, as well as its cultural and artistic influences. A city's art scene can reflect the diversity of its population and its creative energy. Its music scene can be a source of inspiration and pride, showcasing the city's unique rhythms and sounds. Its literature can provide insight into the city's intellectual and creative life, and its food can reflect its cultural diversity and its culinary traditions.

The importance of understanding a city's cultural identity

Understanding a city's cultural identity is essential for several reasons. First, it helps us appreciate the city's diversity and complexity, and it allows us to engage with its residents and communities on a deeper level. Second, it helps us recognize the challenges and opportunities facing the city, from economic inequality to environmental sustainability. Finally, it allows us to learn from the city's history and culture, and to apply those lessons to our own lives and communities.

For example, if we study a city's history of social activism, we may be inspired to get involved in local politics or advocacy work. If we learn about a city's innovative approaches to sustainable development, we may be inspired to apply those approaches in our own communities.

Overview of the book's contents

This book, "Heritage and Culture-Discovering the Heart and Soul of the Capitals," will explore the history and culture of different cities around the world, with a focus on their architecture, art, music, literature, food, festivals, museums, and social dynamics. Each chapter will delve into a specific aspect of a city's cultural identity, providing readers with a comprehensive understanding of what makes each city unique. Through this exploration, we hope to deepen our appreciation for the richness and diversity of our global community, and to gain new insights into the challenges and opportunities facing our world today.

The role of architecture, art, music, literature, food, and festivals in shaping a city's culture cannot be overstated. These various elements serve as a window into a city's soul, and help to define its identity, character, and uniqueness. They are the building blocks that come together to create a rich cultural tapestry that sets a city apart from others.

Architecture is often the first thing that comes to mind when thinking of a city's cultural identity. A city's architecture reflects its history, culture, and values. The design of a city's buildings and public spaces can tell us a lot about the city's priorities and aspirations. For example, the towering skyscrapers of New York City represent its ambition and entrepreneurial spirit, while the winding alleyways and colorful buildings of Havana reflect its rich history and vibrant culture.

Art and music are also integral to a city's cultural identity. A city's art scene is a reflection of its creative spirit and imagination. From street art to galleries, a city's art is an expression of its culture and values. Music is another important aspect of a city's cultural landscape. A city's music scene can be a reflection of its history, its people, and its struggles. For example, New Orleans is known for its jazz music, which reflects the city's African American heritage and its unique blend of cultural influences.

Literature is another important component of a city's cultural identity. A city's literature reflects its history, its people, and its values. From great works of literature to local authors and poets, a city's literature provides insight into its unique cultural heritage. For example, Dublin is known for its literary tradition, which includes famous writers such as James Joyce and W.B. Yeats.

Food is also a critical component of a city's cultural identity. A city's cuisine reflects its history, geography, and culture. From street food to high-end restaurants, a city's food scene is an expression of its unique character and traditions. For example, the street food scene in Bangkok reflects the city's love of spicy and flavorful dishes, while the fine dining scene in Paris reflects its culinary sophistication and refinement.

Finally, festivals and celebrations are an important way in which a city's cultural identity is expressed. Festivals provide a platform for a city to showcase its traditions, music, food, and art. They offer a glimpse into the city's history and culture, and help to create a sense of community and belonging. For example, the Carnival in Rio de Janeiro is an annual celebration that reflects the city's love of music, dance, and pageantry.

In conclusion, the role of architecture, art, music, literature, food, and festivals in shaping a city's culture is vital. These elements come together to create a rich and diverse cultural landscape that reflects a city's history, values, and character. By understanding and appreciating these cultural elements, we can gain a deeper insight into a city's identity, and appreciate the beauty and complexity of its cultural heritage.

Overview of the book's contents

In this book, we will embark on a journey to explore the rich history and diverse cultures that make each capital unique. We will delve into the architecture, art, music, literature, food, and festivals that define each city and uncover the heart and soul of its cultural identity.

Chapter 1 will focus on architecture and landmarks, where we will explore the iconic buildings and structures that have come to represent the city. We will look at the development of different architectural styles over time and understand how public spaces have contributed to the city's identity.

Chapter 2 will cover arts and entertainment, where we will examine the city's artistic traditions and how the art scene has evolved over time. We will explore major cultural institutions, such as museums and theaters, and the city's contributions to local and global music culture. We will also study the role of festivals and celebrations in the city's cultural identity.

Chapter 3 will dive into literature and language, where we will study the city's literary history and famous authors and poets. We will also explore the evolution of the city's language and its linguistic diversity. We will learn about the role of libraries and bookstores in the city's intellectual life and the impact of literature on the city's cultural identity.

Chapter 4 will focus on food and cuisine, where we will examine the city's culinary traditions and famous dishes. We will explore the role of street food and markets in the city's food culture and the impact of immigration on the city's cuisine. We will also study the emergence of new food trends and the city's dining scene.

Chapter 5 will cover festivals and celebrations, where we will study the city's major festivals and their historical and cultural significance. We will explore the role of religion and spirituality in the city's festivals and celebrations and the evolution of the city's festival culture over time. We will also understand the impact of festivals on the city's cultural identity.

Chapter 6 will explore museums and heritage sites, where we will study the city's major museums and heritage sites and their historical and cultural significance. We will understand the role of museums in preserving the city's cultural heritage and the impact of tourism on the city's heritage sites. We will also study the city's approach to preserving and promoting its cultural heritage.

Chapter 7 will focus on culture and society, where we will explore the city's social and cultural diversity and its impact on the city's identity. We will study the role of education and media in shaping the city's cultural landscape and understand the city's cultural policies and initiatives. We will also examine the challenges and opportunities facing the city's cultural sector.

Throughout the book, we will highlight the ways in which these different aspects of a city's culture interact and intersect to create a unique identity. We will also examine the ways in which the city's cultural identity has been shaped by its historical and political context, as well as by its interactions with other cultures around the world. By the end of this book, readers will have a deep understanding of each city's cultural identity and the forces that have shaped it over time.

Chapter 1: Architecture and Landmarks
The city's iconic landmarks and their historical and cultural significance

The city's iconic landmarks are not just structures or buildings, but they are also symbols of the city's identity, history, and culture. They stand as tangible reminders of the city's past, and they also represent the city's aspirations for its future. In this chapter, we will explore some of the most iconic landmarks of the city, and examine their historical and cultural significance.

One of the most recognizable landmarks of the city is the [landmark name]. This [description of landmark] was [built/established] in [year] and has since become a symbol of the city's [attribute or identity]. Its [architectural style] and [unique features] have made it a popular destination for tourists and locals alike. [Historical or cultural significance].

Another iconic landmark of the city is [landmark name]. This [description of landmark] was [built/established] in [year] and has played an important role in the city's history and culture. Its [architectural style] and [unique features] have made it a [must-see destination/a cultural hub]. [Historical or cultural significance].

In addition to these landmarks, the city also boasts several other significant structures and buildings, such as [landmark name], [landmark name], and [landmark name]. Each of these landmarks has its own unique history and cultural significance. For example, [landmark name] was [built/established] in [year] and is known for its [unique features/role in history]. [Historical or cultural significance].

Overall, the city's iconic landmarks are not just important historical and cultural artifacts, but they are also a reflection of the city's people and their values. They represent the city's past, present, and future, and serve as a source of inspiration and pride for generations to come.

The development of architectural styles in the city over time

The development of architectural styles in a city is closely linked to its history, economy, and culture. Over time, a city may experience various architectural styles that reflect different periods, social values, and artistic movements. In this chapter, we will explore the evolution of architectural styles in the city and their cultural significance.

The Early Period: In the early period of the city's development, architecture was primarily influenced by the city's economic and political conditions. During this period, the city's architecture was predominantly characterized by functional buildings and structures that served practical purposes such as defense, transportation, and housing. The earliest examples of architecture in the city were simple structures built with locally sourced materials such as wood, mud, and stone.

Medieval and Renaissance Period: During the Medieval and Renaissance period, the city experienced significant cultural and artistic transformations that were reflected in its architecture. The city's architecture was characterized by the use of decorative elements, such as Gothic arches and stained glass windows, and a focus on symmetry and proportion. Many of the city's most iconic landmarks were constructed during this period, including cathedrals, castles, and city walls. The architecture of this period was a testament to the city's economic and political power and its cultural aspirations.

Baroque and Rococo Period: In the Baroque and Rococo period, the city's architecture became more ornate and elaborate. This style was characterized by curved lines, intricate decoration, and a focus on the dramatic. The city's buildings became more opulent, with ornate facades, grand staircases, and lavish interiors. During this period, the city also experienced significant urbanization, which resulted in the construction of many public buildings such as theaters, opera houses, and palaces.

Modern and Contemporary Period: In the modern and contemporary period, the city's architecture has become more diverse and reflective of its multicultural population. The city's architecture has become more focused on sustainability, with the incorporation of eco-friendly materials and energy-efficient design. The city has also embraced new technologies and innovative designs, resulting in some of the most iconic and futuristic buildings in the world. This period has seen the emergence of skyscrapers, commercial buildings, and modern infrastructure projects that reflect the city's economic and social ambitions.

Conclusion: The development of architectural styles in the city is a reflection of its history, culture, and economic conditions. The city's architecture has evolved over time, reflecting the changing needs and aspirations of its people. Today, the city's architecture is a blend of the old and new, reflecting the city's diverse cultural heritage and its aspirations for the future. The architecture of the city is not only a reflection of its cultural identity, but it also serves as a source of inspiration and pride for its citizens.

The role of public spaces in shaping the city's identity

Public spaces are an essential part of any city's identity. They are the places where people come together to engage in activities, relax, and connect with their community. Public spaces are the physical manifestation of a city's values, priorities, and culture. In this chapter, we will explore the role of public spaces in shaping the identity of a city.

Historically, public spaces have served as gathering places for people from all walks of life. They were the sites of political rallies, protests, and demonstrations, where people came together to voice their opinions and fight for their rights. Public spaces also played a crucial role in the social and cultural life of a city. They were where people went to shop, eat, and socialize.

As cities grew and evolved over time, so too did their public spaces. The design and function of public spaces reflect the needs and aspirations of the people who use them. In many cities, public spaces were reimagined and redesigned to meet the changing demands of urban life.

In some cities, public spaces have become emblematic of the city itself. For example, Central Park in New York City is an iconic public space that is known around the world. The park was designed in the mid-19th century as a place where New Yorkers could escape the noise and chaos of the city. Today, it serves as a beloved green space for millions of people who live and work in the city.

Other cities have their own iconic public spaces that serve as symbols of the city's identity. In Paris, the Champs-Élysées is a famous boulevard that is lined with trees, shops, and cafes. It is a place where people come to see and be seen, to enjoy a coffee or a croissant, and to experience the energy and vitality of Parisian life.

In addition to their cultural significance, public spaces also play an important role in shaping a city's economic and social life. They provide opportunities for businesses to thrive, and they offer a platform for cultural and artistic events. They are also essential for promoting social cohesion and community building.

In recent years, many cities have recognized the importance of public spaces and have invested in their design and maintenance. They have implemented new policies and initiatives aimed at promoting the use and enjoyment of public spaces. For example, some cities have introduced programs to encourage the use of public transportation, cycling, and walking, which in turn, increase the use of public spaces.

In conclusion, public spaces are a crucial part of a city's identity. They reflect the history, culture, and values of the people who use them. They play a vital role in shaping the economic, social, and cultural life of a city. By investing in the design and maintenance of public spaces, cities can create vibrant and inclusive communities that reflect the aspirations and needs of their residents.

The impact of modern architecture on the city's landscape

The post-World War II era marked a significant turning point in the history of architecture, with the advent of modernism and the proliferation of new building materials and construction techniques. This era witnessed the rise of modern architecture, which aimed to break away from traditional design principles and create a new, functional aesthetic.

The impact of modern architecture on the city's landscape cannot be overstated. It has transformed skylines, reshaped cityscapes, and challenged the traditional notions of architecture and design. The use of new materials such as steel and reinforced concrete allowed for taller, more streamlined buildings that could accommodate large numbers of people and businesses. As a result, many cities around the world underwent significant changes in their urban fabric.

One example of the impact of modern architecture on the city's landscape is the skyline of New York City. The city's skyline was forever transformed with the construction of the Empire State Building in 1931, which was then the tallest building in the world. The building's Art Deco design, with its clean lines and geometric shapes, was a significant departure from the ornate styles of the past. It was an instant symbol of modernity and progress and set the stage for the development of skyscrapers around the world.

In addition to changing skylines, modern architecture also transformed the design of public spaces. One example is the High Line in New York City, a public park built on an elevated railroad track. The park is a unique example of how modern architecture can repurpose existing infrastructure to create new public spaces that reflect the city's changing needs and priorities.

Modern architecture has also challenged the traditional notions of what constitutes a building, with some architects blurring the boundaries between buildings and public spaces. One example is the Guggenheim Museum in Bilbao, Spain, designed by Frank Gehry. The museum's undulating titanium-clad structure is a work of art in itself and has become an iconic landmark in the city.

However, the impact of modern architecture has not been without controversy. Some argue that it has led to the destruction of historic buildings and neighborhoods, while others criticize the homogenization of urban landscapes around the world. The use of glass facades and standardized building designs have been criticized for creating sterile, uniform environments that lack the character and charm of older buildings.

In conclusion, the impact of modern architecture on the city's landscape has been significant, transforming skylines, reshaping public spaces, and challenging traditional notions of architecture and design. While it has brought many benefits, it has also faced criticism for its role in the destruction of historic buildings and the homogenization of urban landscapes. As cities continue to evolve and grow, the role of modern architecture in shaping their identity will remain a subject of debate and discussion.

Chapter 2: Arts and Entertainment
The city's artistic traditions and the evolution of its art scene

Art has been an integral part of the city's cultural heritage, reflecting the city's history and the values of its people. From ancient times to the present day, the city has produced a wealth of artistic expressions in various mediums, including painting, sculpture, ceramics, and textiles.

The city's artistic traditions date back thousands of years, and archaeological excavations have revealed that the city was a major center of art production during the ancient times. The city's art was heavily influenced by the surrounding regions, particularly by the art of neighboring cities and countries. For example, during the 2nd millennium BC, the city was part of the Hittite Empire, and the art of that era is characterized by a mix of Hittite, Mesopotamian, and Egyptian styles.

During the Middle Ages, the city was a melting pot of various cultures, resulting in a vibrant and diverse art scene. The city's artists produced works in a wide range of styles, from Byzantine and Islamic art to European Renaissance and Baroque art. Many of the city's medieval churches and monasteries feature elaborate frescoes, mosaics, and icons that showcase the city's artistic heritage.

The city's modern art scene emerged in the late 19th and early 20th centuries, influenced by the global art movements of the time, such as Impressionism, Expressionism, and Cubism. The city's artists embraced these new styles and incorporated them into their works, creating a unique fusion of local and global artistic expressions.

In the mid-20th century, the city's art scene experienced a major transformation with the emergence of Abstract Expressionism. The city became a hub for avant-garde artists who sought to break away from traditional art forms and experiment with new materials and techniques. Many of these artists gained international recognition, and their works are now part of major museum collections around the world.

Today, the city's art scene continues to evolve, with new generations of artists exploring new mediums and pushing the boundaries of traditional art forms. The city is home to numerous art galleries, museums, and art festivals, providing a platform for local and international artists to showcase their works.

In conclusion, the city's artistic traditions have played a vital role in shaping its cultural identity, reflecting its history, diversity, and values. The city's art scene has evolved over the centuries, adapting to new influences and emerging as a vibrant and dynamic cultural force.

The major cultural institutions in the city, such as museums and theaters

Museums and theaters are integral to the cultural life of a city, as they provide a space for people to engage with art, history, and culture. Museums serve as repositories of a city's history and cultural heritage, while theaters provide a venue for the performing arts, including theater, dance, and music. In this chapter, we will explore some of the major cultural institutions in the city, and their role in shaping the city's cultural identity.

Museums

Museums play a crucial role in preserving a city's cultural heritage and providing educational opportunities for its citizens. They are also important tourist attractions, drawing visitors from around the world to experience the city's art and history. In the following sections, we will highlight some of the major museums in the city, and their contributions to the cultural landscape.

Art Museums

Art museums are among the most popular types of museums in the world, and the city boasts several world-class institutions. The city's art museums feature collections of both contemporary and historical art, and their exhibitions often attract large crowds. The museums' collections reflect the city's diverse cultural heritage, with works from local, national, and international artists.

One of the city's most renowned art museums is the XYZ Museum, which houses a vast collection of contemporary art from around the world. The museum's collection includes works by some of the most influential artists of the 20th and 21st centuries, such as Pablo Picasso, Jackson Pollock, and Andy Warhol. The museum also hosts temporary exhibitions that showcase emerging artists and contemporary art movements.

History Museums

History museums provide visitors with an opportunity to learn about the city's past and the people who shaped it. They often feature interactive exhibits and artifacts that bring history to life. In the city, there are several history museums that cover a range of topics, from the city's founding to its role in shaping national and international events.

One of the most important history museums in the city is the XYZ History Museum, which chronicles the city's history from its founding to the present day. The museum's exhibits include artifacts, photographs, and documents that tell the story of the city's development and its cultural and political milestones. The museum also hosts special exhibitions that explore specific topics, such as the city's role in the Civil Rights movement.

Theaters

Theaters are essential to the city's cultural life, as they provide a platform for the performing arts, including theater, dance, and music. The city has a long history of supporting the performing arts, and its theaters have hosted some of the world's most renowned performers. In this section, we will highlight some of the city's major theaters and their contributions to the cultural landscape.

Broadway Theaters

The city is home to some of the most famous theaters in the world, located in the heart of the Theater District on Broadway. The Broadway theaters are known for their lavish productions, featuring some of the world's most talented actors, directors, and designers. Broadway shows draw audiences from around the world and are an important part of the city's cultural identity.

One of the most famous Broadway theaters is the XYZ Theater, which has hosted some of the most successful shows in Broadway history. The theater's ornate architecture and luxurious interiors make it a popular destination for theatergoers. The XYZ Theater has been a fixture in the city's cultural landscape for over a century, and its productions continue to draw audiences from around the world.

Off-Broadway Theaters

In addition to the Broadway theaters, the city is also home to a thriving off-Broadway theater scene. Off-Broadway theaters offer a more intimate and experimental approach to theater, often showcasing emerging playwrights and performers. Off-B-Broadway theaters typically have smaller seating capacities than their Broadway counterparts, creating a more immersive experience for the audience. Some of the most popular off-Broadway theaters in the city include the Public Theater, the Vineyard Theatre, and the New York Theatre Workshop. These theaters have a long history of producing groundbreaking shows that have gone on to achieve critical acclaim and commercial success.

Another major cultural institution in the city is the Metropolitan Museum of Art, commonly referred to as the "Met." Located on Fifth Avenue, the Met is one of the largest and most comprehensive art museums in the world, with a collection spanning over 5,000 years of art from all around the globe. The museum's collection includes everything from ancient Egyptian artifacts to contemporary works of art, and attracts millions of visitors each year.

In addition to the Met, the city is also home to a number of other world-renowned museums, including the Museum of Modern Art (MoMA), the Solomon R. Guggenheim Museum, and the Whitney Museum of American Art. These museums showcase some of the most important and influential works of art from around the world, and are a must-visit for any art lover visiting the city.

The city's rich cultural landscape also includes a thriving music scene, with a wide variety of genres represented. Some of the most famous music venues in the city include Carnegie Hall, the Apollo Theater, and Madison Square Garden. These venues have hosted some of the biggest names in music, from classical virtuosos to rock legends.

Finally, the city's film scene is also a major cultural force, with numerous film festivals and cinemas showcasing some of the best independent and international films. The most famous of these festivals is the Tribeca Film Festival, founded by Robert De Niro, which brings together filmmakers and film lovers from around the world to celebrate the art of cinema. The city also has a number of historic movie theaters, such as the Ziegfeld Theatre and the Paris Theatre, which add to the city's cinematic heritage.

The city's music scene and its contributions to local and global music culture

New York City has a rich and diverse music scene that has contributed significantly to both local and global music culture. From jazz and hip-hop to classical and opera, the city's music scene offers a wide range of genres and styles.

One of the city's most significant contributions to music culture is jazz. Harlem, a neighborhood in the northern part of Manhattan, is considered the birthplace of jazz. During the Harlem Renaissance in the 1920s, jazz flourished, and musicians such as Duke Ellington, Louis Armstrong, and Ella Fitzgerald performed at local clubs and theaters. Today, jazz is still alive and well in the city, with venues like the Village Vanguard and the Blue Note showcasing both established and up-and-coming jazz musicians.

Hip-hop is another genre that originated in New York City, specifically in the Bronx in the late 1970s. The genre's roots can be traced back to block parties where DJs would play and remix funk and soul records, and MCs would rap over the music. Hip-hop quickly became a cultural phenomenon and has since become a global music genre. The city's contribution to hip-hop culture can be seen in the many hip-hop museums and tours, as well as the annual Hip-Hop Honors event.

Classical music also has a strong presence in the city, with institutions like the Metropolitan Opera House and Carnegie Hall hosting world-renowned orchestras and performers. The Metropolitan Opera House, located in Lincoln Center, has been the home of the Metropolitan Opera since it opened in 1966. Carnegie Hall, located in Midtown Manhattan, has been a venue for classical music performances since it opened in 1891.

In addition to these well-known genres, the city's music scene also includes a range of other styles, such as salsa, reggae, and punk rock. The city's diversity is reflected in its music, with many immigrant communities bringing their own musical traditions and styles to the city.

The city's music scene has not only contributed to local culture but has also had a significant impact on global music culture. Many musicians who got their start in the city, such as Jay-Z, Nas, and Alicia Keys, have become global music icons. The city's influence can also be seen in the many music festivals and events that take place throughout the year, such as the Governors Ball Music Festival and the SummerStage concert series.

Overall, the city's music scene is an essential part of its cultural identity and has contributed significantly to both local and global music culture.

The role of festivals and celebrations in the city's cultural identity

Festivals and celebrations play an integral role in shaping the cultural identity of a city, and this is especially true in the case of New York City. The city hosts a plethora of festivals and celebrations throughout the year, representing the diversity of its population and its rich cultural heritage.

One of the most iconic festivals in New York City is the Macy's Thanksgiving Day Parade. This annual event has been held since 1924 and attracts millions of viewers from around the world. The parade features giant balloons, floats, and performances by musicians and other entertainers.

Another major festival in the city is the Chinese New Year parade, which celebrates the Lunar New Year and features traditional Chinese dragon and lion dances, as well as performances by Chinese musicians and dancers. The parade is one of the largest celebrations of its kind outside of Asia and attracts thousands of visitors each year.

The New York City Pride Parade is also a significant event that celebrates the LGBTQ+ community and its contributions to the city's culture. The parade features floats, performances, and marches by LGBTQ+ organizations and individuals, as well as allies and supporters.

Other notable festivals in the city include the West Indian Day Parade, which celebrates Caribbean culture, and the Feast of San Gennaro, which celebrates Italian heritage and features traditional Italian food and music.

These festivals not only provide entertainment and enjoyment for the city's residents and visitors, but also serve as a means of promoting cultural exchange and understanding. They showcase the diversity of the city's population and serve as a reminder of the importance of embracing and celebrating different cultures.

In addition to these major festivals, there are countless smaller celebrations and events that take place throughout the city. These include street fairs, neighborhood block parties, and cultural festivals that celebrate specific ethnic or national groups.

Overall, the festivals and celebrations in New York City are an essential component of its cultural identity. They provide a means of celebrating and showcasing the city's diversity, promoting cultural exchange and understanding, and fostering a sense of community among its residents.

Chapter 3: Literature and Language
The city's literary history and its famous authors and poets

The city has a rich literary history, and it has been home to some of the world's most celebrated authors and poets. Many literary movements have originated in the city, and its literary culture continues to thrive to this day. One of the most famous literary movements to emerge from the city was the Harlem Renaissance, which took place in the 1920s and 1930s. This movement was characterized by a flourishing of African American literature, music, and art, and it produced some of the most significant works of literature of the 20th century.

One of the most famous authors associated with the city is F. Scott Fitzgerald, who is best known for his novel "The Great Gatsby." Fitzgerald lived and worked in the city during the 1920s, and he wrote extensively about the city's social scene and the excesses of the Jazz Age. Other notable authors who lived and worked in the city include Ernest Hemingway, James Baldwin, Langston Hughes, Edith Wharton, and Herman Melville.

The city has also been home to some of the world's most famous poets. Walt Whitman, one of the most influential poets in American literature, lived and worked in the city for many years, and his poetry is closely associated with the city. Other famous poets associated with the city include Langston Hughes, Allen Ginsberg, and Frank O'Hara.

The city has also been the setting for many famous works of literature. Some of the most notable include "The Catcher in the Rye" by J.D. Salinger, "Invisible Man" by Ralph Ellison, and "The Bonfire of the Vanities" by Tom Wolfe. These works capture the city's energy and its many contradictions, and they continue to resonate with readers today.

Overall, the city's literary history is an essential part of its cultural identity, and it continues to inspire writers and readers around the world. The city's many literary landmarks, including libraries, bookstores, and literary festivals, are a testament to its rich literary tradition.

The evolution of the city's language and its linguistic diversity

The city's linguistic diversity is one of its defining features. From its earliest days, the city has been a melting pot of cultures and languages. The first European settlers spoke Dutch, but soon English became the dominant language. However, other languages and dialects have been present in the city since its inception.

In the 19th century, waves of immigrants arrived from all over the world, bringing with them their native languages and dialects. As a result, the city became a center for multilingualism, with neighborhoods and enclaves where people spoke everything from Yiddish to Italian to Chinese. This diversity of languages has only grown over time, with newer waves of immigrants adding their languages to the mix.

One of the most significant developments in the city's linguistic landscape has been the rise of Spanish. Today, Spanish is the second most commonly spoken language in the city, after English. This is due in part to the large number of Latin American immigrants who have settled in the city since the 1960s. In some neighborhoods, such as Washington Heights and the South Bronx, Spanish is the primary language spoken.

Other languages that are widely spoken in the city include Chinese, Russian, and various South Asian languages. There are also many smaller communities of speakers of languages like Bengali, Arabic, and Korean. This linguistic diversity has had a profound impact on the city's culture and identity, shaping everything from its cuisine to its music to its literature.

The city's linguistic diversity is also reflected in its literature. Many of the city's most famous writers have been immigrants or the children of immigrants, and their work reflects the linguistic and cultural complexity of the city. For example, the works of authors like Junot Diaz and Edwidge Danticat draw on their experiences growing up in immigrant communities, and incorporate Spanish and Creole words and phrases into their writing.

In recent years, there has been a renewed interest in preserving and promoting the city's linguistic diversity. Organizations like the Center for World Languages and Cultures at New York University and the Endangered Language Alliance work to document and support the city's many endangered languages. These efforts recognize the importance of language in shaping the city's cultural identity and ensuring its future as a center of linguistic diversity.

The role of libraries and bookstores in the city's intellectual life

Libraries and bookstores have played a significant role in shaping the intellectual life of cities throughout history, and this is especially true in the case of the city we are discussing. The city boasts some of the world's most impressive libraries, including the famous New York Public Library, the Brooklyn Public Library, and the Columbia University Libraries. These institutions have been critical to the preservation and dissemination of knowledge, literature, and history, as well as serving as important community gathering places.

The New York Public Library is one of the most iconic buildings in the city and houses over 53 million items, including books, manuscripts, and maps. The library's collection includes rare and valuable books, such as a Gutenberg Bible, as well as manuscripts from some of the world's most celebrated authors, including Virginia Woolf, Franz Kafka, and Albert Einstein. The library's main reading room is a breathtaking space, with tall ceilings, chandeliers, and rows of wooden tables and chairs, where scholars, writers, and visitors can come to read, study, and work.

Bookstores, too, have played a vital role in the city's intellectual and cultural life. From the legendary Strand

Bookstore to independent bookstores like McNally Jackson and Greenlight Bookstore, the city is home to a diverse range of bookstores, each with its unique character and selection of books. These bookstores have served as a vital resource for bibliophiles and a hub for literary events, author readings, and book clubs. They have also played a critical role in supporting the city's independent publishing industry, which has been responsible for publishing some of the most significant works of literature in recent times.

Moreover, the city's libraries and bookstores have played a critical role in promoting literacy and education in the city's diverse communities. The New York Public Library, for example, has a robust outreach program that provides services to people who are unable to visit the library in person, including homebound individuals, incarcerated people, and students. Similarly, many independent bookstores have programs that support community literacy efforts, such as donating books to schools and libraries and hosting reading programs for children.

In conclusion, libraries and bookstores have played an essential role in shaping the intellectual and cultural life of the city. They have served as gathering places for communities, preserved and disseminated knowledge, and promoted literacy and education. The city's libraries and bookstores have played a critical role in fostering intellectual curiosity and creativity and have been vital resources for writers, scholars, and readers alike.

The impact of literature on the city's cultural identity

The impact of literature on a city's cultural identity cannot be overstated. Literature reflects a city's values, beliefs, and experiences, and it has the power to shape how outsiders view the city and how locals see themselves. In this chapter, we will explore the impact of literature on the cultural identity of our city.

Firstly, we will examine the ways in which literature can capture the essence of a city. Our city has been the setting for countless novels, short stories, and poems, each of which provides a unique perspective on its people, places, and events. From the gritty realism of urban noir to the lyrical beauty of poetry, these works of literature offer a window into the soul of our city and the experiences of its inhabitants.

Secondly, we will look at the role of literature in shaping our city's identity. Over the years, our city has produced a number of famous authors who have contributed to the literary canon of our country. Their works have not only brought our city to the attention of the wider world but have also helped to define what it means to be a resident of our city. We will explore the works of these authors and the impact they have had on our city's identity.

Thirdly, we will consider the ways in which literature can inspire cultural change. Literature has the power to challenge and transform the status quo, and many works of literature have been instrumental in advancing social and political causes. Our city has a rich history of literary activism, with authors and poets often at the forefront of struggles for social justice and equality. We will examine some of the most influential works of literature to emerge from these movements and the ways in which they have helped to shape our city's cultural identity.

Finally, we will look at the ways in which literature can inspire community building and promote a sense of shared identity. Literature can bring people together, providing a common ground for conversation and connection. Our city is home to a vibrant literary community, with numerous book clubs, reading groups, and literary events taking place throughout the year. We will explore the ways in which these activities contribute to our city's cultural identity and help to foster a sense of community among its residents.

In conclusion, literature plays a crucial role in shaping a city's cultural identity. It captures the essence of a place, defines its values and beliefs, inspires social and political change, and brings people together. By exploring the impact of literature on our city, we can gain a deeper understanding of what makes it unique and what unites us as its residents.

Chapter 4: Food and Cuisine
The city's culinary traditions and famous dishes

New York City is a melting pot of cultures, and its culinary scene reflects this diversity. The city's food culture has been shaped by the many immigrant communities that have settled there over the years. Each community has brought its own unique culinary traditions, and over time, these traditions have merged to create a vibrant and dynamic food scene.

One of the most iconic dishes associated with New York City is the pizza. New York-style pizza is known for its thin, crispy crust, and its large, foldable slices. The city is home to many pizzerias that have become legendary, including Lombardi's, which is widely regarded as the first pizzeria in the United States.

Another famous dish associated with the city is the bagel. New York-style bagels are known for their chewy texture and are often topped with cream cheese and lox. The city is home to many famous bagel shops, including Russ & Daughters and H&H Bagels.

The city is also known for its hot dogs, which are typically topped with mustard and sauerkraut. Nathan's Famous is a well-known hot dog chain that originated in Coney Island and has become a cultural icon in the city.

Beyond these iconic dishes, the city's food scene offers a wide range of culinary experiences. The city's many neighborhoods each have their own unique food scenes, offering everything from traditional Chinese dim sum in Chinatown to authentic Italian cuisine in Little Italy.

New York City is also home to many famous restaurants, including the Michelin-starred Eleven Madison Park and Per Se. These restaurants offer world-class dining experiences and are known for their innovative and creative menus.

Overall, the city's culinary traditions are an important part of its cultural identity. The many diverse cuisines that can be found throughout the city reflect the city's history and the many different communities that have settled there. Whether it's a slice of pizza, a bagel with lox, or a fancy tasting menu at a Michelin-starred restaurant, New York City's food culture is sure to leave a lasting impression.

The role of street food and markets in the city's food culture

The bustling streets of the city are not only home to towering skyscrapers and iconic landmarks, but also to a rich and diverse street food culture. From hot dogs and pretzels to tacos and kebabs, street food vendors offer a glimpse into the city's culinary traditions and serve as an integral part of its food culture.

Street food has a long and rich history in the city. The first hot dog stand was established in Coney Island in the 1860s, and by the early 1900s, the city was home to a vibrant street food scene. In the decades that followed, street food vendors would go on to introduce a variety of international flavors to the city, from falafel and gyros to dim sum and sushi.

Today, street food remains an essential part of the city's food culture, with vendors offering a diverse range of dishes from all corners of the globe. One of the most iconic street food items in the city is the hot dog, which can be found on street corners and at sporting events throughout the city. The hot dog has become so ingrained in the city's culture that it has even inspired its own style of preparation: the New York-style hot dog, which is typically served with sauerkraut, onions, and mustard.

Other popular street food items in the city include pretzels, pizza, tacos, falafel, and kebabs. Many of these dishes have been adapted to suit the city's unique taste preferences, with variations such as the "slice" pizza, which is sold by the slice rather than by the pie, and the "halal cart" chicken and rice dish, which has become a staple of the city's street food scene.

In addition to the city's street food vendors, its many markets also play a significant role in shaping its food culture. One of the most iconic markets in the city is the Chelsea Market, which is housed in a former Nabisco factory and is home to a variety of food vendors, artisanal food producers, and restaurants. The market offers visitors a chance to sample a wide range of local and international cuisine, from sushi and ramen to lobster rolls and artisanal cheese.

Another famous market in the city is the Union Square Greenmarket, which operates year-round and features over 140 regional farmers, fishermen, and bakers. The market offers a wide range of fresh produce, meats, cheeses, and baked goods, and has become a popular destination for foodies and chefs alike.

Beyond the Chelsea Market and Union Square Greenmarket, the city is also home to a variety of other markets and food halls, such as Smorgasburg and Time Out Market. These markets offer visitors a chance to sample a wide range of dishes from some of the city's most innovative and up-and-coming chefs and food vendors.

In recent years, the city's street food and market culture has undergone a revival, with many vendors and markets embracing sustainable and locally sourced ingredients, as well as innovative cooking techniques and flavors. The city's food culture continues to evolve and adapt to new trends and tastes, but its vibrant street food scene and bustling markets remain an integral part of its cultural identity.

The impact of immigration on the city's cuisine

New York City's cuisine is heavily influenced by the waves of immigrants who have settled in the city throughout its history. The city's cuisine is a reflection of the diverse cultural groups that have made New York their home. The cuisine of the city is a result of the blending of different culinary traditions from around the world.

The early 19th century saw an influx of Irish immigrants, who brought with them their love of potatoes and corned beef. They settled in areas like Hell's Kitchen and the Lower East Side. These areas would later become famous for their Irish pubs and restaurants.

Later in the century, Italian immigrants began to arrive in large numbers. They brought with them their love of pasta, pizza, and red sauce. Italian cuisine has had a huge influence on the city's food scene, and Italian-American dishes like spaghetti and meatballs and chicken Parmesan have become beloved staples.

The 20th century brought even more waves of immigration, and with it came new and exciting flavors. Jewish immigrants introduced bagels, lox, and pastrami sandwiches. Chinese immigrants brought dim sum and other Cantonese specialties. Puerto Rican immigrants brought with them their love of plantains, yucca, and pork.

Today, New York City's food scene continues to be shaped by its immigrant communities. The city's diverse neighborhoods are home to a wide variety of ethnic restaurants and food markets, offering everything from traditional Mexican street food to authentic Korean barbecue.

One notable example is the Little Italy neighborhood in Manhattan, which was once a predominantly Italian-American area. Today, the area has become more diverse, with restaurants serving cuisines from all over the world. However, it still maintains its Italian roots, with many classic Italian restaurants and bakeries still in operation.

Immigrants have also introduced new culinary techniques and ingredients to the city. For example, Mexican immigrants have introduced the use of chili peppers and avocado in many dishes, while Thai immigrants have brought the flavors of lemongrass and coconut milk.

Overall, the impact of immigration on New York City's cuisine cannot be overstated. The city's food scene is a reflection of its diverse population, and the culinary traditions that have been introduced by immigrants continue to shape the city's food culture.

The city's dining scene and the emergence of new food trends

New York City has long been a hub for culinary experimentation and innovation, with chefs and restaurateurs constantly pushing the boundaries of traditional cuisine. The city's dining scene is constantly evolving, with new trends emerging each year.

One trend that has taken the city by storm in recent years is the farm-to-table movement. This movement emphasizes the use of locally-sourced, seasonal ingredients in cooking, with the goal of promoting sustainability and supporting local farmers. Many restaurants in the city have embraced this movement, featuring farm-fresh produce and sustainably-raised meats on their menus.

Another emerging trend in the city's dining scene is the rise of plant-based cuisine. As more people become aware of the environmental and health benefits of a plant-based diet, restaurants are responding by offering more vegetarian and vegan options. Some restaurants have even gone completely plant-based, offering menus that are entirely free of animal products.

In addition to these new trends, New York City's dining scene continues to be influenced by its diverse immigrant population. Immigrants have brought with them a wide range of cuisines from around the world, from Italian and Chinese to Mexican and Middle Eastern. Many of these cuisines have become an integral part of the city's food culture, with numerous restaurants offering authentic and delicious takes on dishes from different countries and regions.

The city's dining scene is also shaped by its high-end restaurants and celebrity chefs. Many of the world's top chefs have restaurants in New York City, and these restaurants are known for their exceptional cuisine, innovative cooking techniques, and sophisticated atmospheres. These high-end restaurants often set the standard for dining trends and culinary innovation, inspiring chefs and foodies around the world.

Overall, New York City's dining scene is a reflection of its diverse population, its commitment to sustainability and innovation, and its reputation as a cultural hub. With new trends and cuisines emerging each year, the city's dining scene is sure to continue to surprise and delight food lovers from around the world.

Chapter 5: Festivals and Celebrations
The city's major festivals and celebrations and their historical and cultural significance

New York City is home to a variety of festivals and celebrations that showcase the city's diversity and cultural richness. From the Chinese New Year Parade to the Pride Parade, there is always something to celebrate in New York. In this section, we will explore some of the major festivals and celebrations in the city and their historical and cultural significance.

One of the most iconic events in New York City is the Macy's Thanksgiving Day Parade. First held in 1924, the parade attracts millions of viewers each year and features giant balloons, floats, marching bands, and performances. The parade is a celebration of Thanksgiving and the start of the holiday season and is a significant part of American culture.

Another major event is the New Year's Eve Ball Drop in Times Square. Millions of people gather in Times Square to watch the ball drop at midnight and ring in the new year. The tradition started in 1907 and has become a worldwide symbol of New Year's Eve celebrations.

The Chinese New Year Parade is another significant event in New York City's festival calendar. The parade celebrates the lunar new year and features dragon and lion dances, traditional Chinese music, and other performances. The event attracts thousands of spectators and is a symbol of the city's diverse cultural heritage.

The Pride Parade is another notable event in the city's festival calendar. The parade celebrates the LGBTQ+ community and their contributions to society. It features floats, performers, and activists marching through the streets of Manhattan, promoting equality and acceptance. The Pride Parade is a symbol of the city's progressive and inclusive values.

The West Indian Day Parade is another significant event in the city's festival calendar. The parade celebrates Caribbean culture and features colorful costumes, music, and dancing. It is held annually on Labor Day and attracts thousands of participants and spectators.

The Feast of San Gennaro is another significant event in the city's festival calendar. The feast is a celebration of Italian culture and heritage and features street vendors selling traditional Italian food, games, and carnival rides. The feast has been held annually in Little Italy since 1926 and is one of the city's oldest and most beloved events.

In conclusion, the festivals and celebrations in New York City are an essential part of its cultural identity. They celebrate the city's diversity, cultural heritage, and values and bring people together from all walks of life. These events showcase the city's vibrancy and creativity and are a testament to the resilience and spirit of New Yorkers.

The role of religion and spirituality in the city's festivals and celebrations

The city's festivals and celebrations are often rooted in religious and spiritual traditions, reflecting the city's diverse cultural and religious landscape. Religion plays a significant role in shaping the city's identity and is often intertwined with its history, architecture, and art. Many of the city's festivals and celebrations have their roots in religious or spiritual practices, and these events often serve as a way for people to connect with their faith and with each other.

One of the most significant religious festivals in the city is Easter, which is celebrated by many of the city's Christian communities. The annual Easter Parade and Bonnet Festival takes place on Fifth Avenue, with people donning colorful and elaborate hats and parading down the street. The festival has its roots in the Catholic celebration of Easter and has become a popular event for people of all faiths and backgrounds to participate in.

Another important religious festival in the city is Diwali, the Hindu festival of lights. The festival is celebrated by the city's large Indian community and marks the triumph of good over evil. During Diwali, the streets are lit up with colorful lights, and people exchange sweets and gifts with each other. The festival is an opportunity for people to come together to celebrate their culture and heritage.

In addition to religious festivals, the city is also home to a number of spiritual celebrations that reflect the city's diverse landscape. The African American Day Parade, for example, is a celebration of the city's black heritage and culture. The parade features music, dance, and other performances that showcase the contributions of the city's African American community.

The city's festivals and celebrations are also an important way for people to connect with each other and to celebrate their shared humanity. The Pride Parade, for example, is a celebration of the city's LGBTQ+ community and serves as a powerful symbol of acceptance and inclusivity. The parade brings together people from all walks of life to celebrate diversity and promote equality.

Religion and spirituality play an important role in shaping the city's festivals and celebrations, but these events are also an opportunity for people to come together to celebrate their shared humanity. The city's diverse cultural and religious landscape is reflected in its festivals and celebrations, making them an important part of the city's cultural identity.

The evolution of the city's festival culture over time

The city's festival culture has undergone significant changes over time, reflecting shifts in the city's demographics, social structures, and cultural influences. The early history of the city's festivals was largely centered around religious observances, with holidays such as Easter, Christmas, and Hanukkah being celebrated by the respective communities. As the city grew and became more diverse, new festivals and celebrations emerged, reflecting the changing demographics and cultural influences.

One significant event that marked a shift in the city's festival culture was the 1964 World's Fair, which was held in Queens. The fair showcased different countries and their cultures, and had a profound impact on the city's cultural landscape. It not only brought attention to the city's multiculturalism, but also inspired the creation of new festivals and celebrations that celebrated the city's diversity.

In the 1970s and 1980s, the city experienced a cultural renaissance that led to the emergence of new festivals that celebrated different aspects of the city's identity. One of the most famous of these is the West Indian Day Parade, which was founded in 1969 and celebrates the Caribbean culture and heritage of the city. Other festivals that emerged during this time included the Chinese New Year Parade, the Puerto

Rican Day Parade, and the Greenwich Village Halloween Parade, which celebrates the city's bohemian and artistic communities.

The 1990s saw the emergence of new festivals that celebrated the city's culinary traditions and food culture. One of the most popular of these is the annual New York City Wine and Food Festival, which attracts some of the top chefs and culinary experts from around the world. The festival also features a range of culinary events, such as tastings, cooking demonstrations, and panel discussions on food-related topics.

In recent years, the city's festival culture has continued to evolve and adapt to changing social and cultural trends. The COVID-19 pandemic had a significant impact on the city's festivals and celebrations, with many events being canceled or moved online. However, the city has found ways to adapt, with many festivals creating virtual experiences that allow people to participate from home.

Overall, the evolution of the city's festival culture reflects the diverse and ever-changing nature of the city itself. From religious observances to celebrations of cultural diversity and culinary traditions, the city's festivals and celebrations continue to play a vital role in shaping the city's cultural identity and bringing people together in celebration.

The impact of festivals on the city's cultural identity is significant and multifaceted. Festivals have the power to bring together people from diverse backgrounds and cultures, celebrating their shared experiences and creating a sense of community. They serve as a platform for showcasing and promoting the city's art, music, literature, and culinary traditions to locals and visitors alike.

One of the most significant impacts of festivals is their role in preserving and promoting cultural heritage. Festivals often serve as a means of passing down cultural traditions and practices from one generation to the next. In many cases, they provide an opportunity for people to reconnect with their cultural roots and identity, especially for diaspora communities.

For example, the New York City Caribbean Carnival, also known as the West Indian Day Parade, is a vibrant celebration of Caribbean culture that has been held in Brooklyn since 1969. The parade and associated events showcase the food, music, dance, and fashion of the Caribbean region, including Trinidad and Tobago, Jamaica, Barbados, and Haiti. For many Caribbean immigrants and their descendants, the festival serves as a way to connect with their cultural heritage and celebrate their identity.

Festivals also contribute to the city's economy by generating revenue from tourism and promoting local businesses. Major events such as the Macy's Thanksgiving Day Parade, New York Fashion Week, and the Tribeca Film Festival attract visitors from all over the world, boosting the city's tourism industry and generating significant economic benefits. Additionally, local vendors, food trucks, and restaurants benefit from increased foot traffic during festivals and celebrations.

Festivals also have a significant impact on the city's cultural landscape, creating a sense of place and enhancing the city's reputation as a cultural hub. Festivals and celebrations, such as the Lunar New Year Parade and the Puerto Rican Day Parade, serve as important cultural touchstones for the city's diverse communities, highlighting their contributions to the city's history and identity.

Finally, festivals and celebrations can serve as a platform for social and political activism, bringing attention to important issues and promoting social change. For example, the Pride Parade, held annually in June, serves as a celebration of LGBTQ+ culture and history, as well as a reminder of the ongoing struggle for equality and acceptance. The parade has played an important role in raising awareness of LGBTQ+ issues and advocating for social change.

In conclusion, festivals and celebrations have a profound impact on the city's cultural identity, economy, and social and political landscape. They serve as a means of promoting cultural heritage, connecting diverse communities, and creating a sense of place and belonging. The evolution of festival culture in New York City reflects the city's ongoing transformation and adaptation to changing social and cultural dynamics.

Chapter 6: Museums and Heritage Sites
The city's major museums and heritage sites and their historical and cultural significance

New York City is home to some of the world's most famous museums and heritage sites, each with its unique story and cultural significance. From the iconic Metropolitan Museum of Art to the moving National September 11 Memorial and Museum, these institutions are vital to the city's cultural identity.

The Metropolitan Museum of Art, commonly known as "the Met," is one of the largest and most comprehensive art museums in the world. Founded in 1870, the museum houses over two million works of art from around the globe, spanning more than 5,000 years of human history. The museum's collections range from ancient Egyptian artifacts to contemporary art, including paintings, sculptures, decorative arts, and photography. The Met's vast collection and extensive exhibitions make it a must-visit destination for art lovers and tourists alike.

Another iconic museum in the city is the American Museum of Natural History. Founded in 1869, the museum is dedicated to exploring the natural world and human cultures. The museum is home to over 33 million specimens and artifacts, including fossils, minerals, and cultural artifacts from around the world. The museum's most famous exhibit is the Rose Center for Earth and Space, which features a planetarium and exhibits about the universe and our place in it.

The 9/11 Memorial and Museum is a moving tribute to the victims of the September 11, 2001 terrorist attacks on the World Trade Center. The memorial features two reflecting pools, each on the footprint of one of the towers, surrounded by a park-like setting. The museum, located underground, tells the story of the attacks and their aftermath through artifacts, personal stories, and interactive exhibits. The 9/11 Memorial and Museum is a powerful reminder of the resilience of the human spirit and the importance of remembering and honoring those who lost their lives.

In addition to these iconic institutions, the city is home to a wide range of smaller museums and heritage sites that showcase the diverse history and culture of New York. The Lower East Side Tenement Museum tells the story of immigrants who lived in the tenement building at 97 Orchard Street, highlighting the struggles and triumphs of working-class families from around the world. The Studio Museum in Harlem celebrates the rich artistic traditions of the Harlem community, featuring exhibitions and programs focused on African American art and culture.

Overall, the city's museums and heritage sites are integral to its cultural identity and offer visitors a unique perspective on the history and diversity of New York City. From the grand halls of the Met to the personal stories told at the Tenement Museum, these institutions tell the story of the city and its people.

The role of museums in preserving the city's cultural heritage

Museums play an essential role in preserving a city's cultural heritage. They act as a repository of artifacts and documents that provide insights into the city's past, and they serve as an educational resource for current and future generations. In this section, we will explore the role of museums in preserving the cultural heritage of the city.

Museums collect, store, and exhibit a wide range of artifacts, from archaeological finds to contemporary art. They serve as a resource for researchers, students, and anyone interested in learning about the city's history and culture. They provide opportunities for visitors to explore the past and learn about the cultural traditions and practices of the city.

Museums play an important role in preserving the cultural heritage of the city. They act as a storehouse of information, preserving and safeguarding the city's cultural and historical artifacts. These artifacts can include documents, photographs, art, and artifacts from daily life. They provide invaluable insights into the city's history, customs, and traditions.

Museums also play a critical role in education. They provide a platform for learning about the city's cultural heritage and history, making it accessible to a wide audience. By providing educational programming, including tours, workshops, and lectures, museums help visitors gain a deeper understanding of the city's culture and history.

Museums also provide an opportunity for communities to engage with their cultural heritage actively. They provide a space for communities to come together and celebrate their cultural traditions and practices. Through exhibitions and events, museums can help promote cultural diversity and encourage cross-cultural understanding.

In addition to preserving the city's cultural heritage, museums also contribute to the economy. They attract visitors from around the world and create jobs in the local economy. Museums can also help revitalize neighborhoods by attracting businesses and tourists to the area.

Overall, museums play a critical role in preserving the cultural heritage of the city. They provide opportunities for education, community engagement, and economic development. Through their exhibitions and programming, museums help promote cross-cultural understanding and encourage the celebration of cultural diversity.

The impact of tourism on the city's heritage sites

Introduction: Tourism can have a significant impact on the preservation and presentation of heritage sites in a city. While tourism can provide valuable resources for the maintenance and development of heritage sites, it can also present challenges in terms of conservation, visitor management, and authenticity. This section will explore the impact of tourism on the city's heritage sites, both positive and negative, and will examine ways in which the city can manage tourism to maximize its benefits while minimizing its drawbacks.

Positive impact of tourism on heritage sites: Tourism can bring significant economic benefits to heritage sites. Increased tourism can generate revenue for the site and the surrounding area, providing resources for the maintenance and restoration of the site. In addition, tourism can create jobs in the tourism industry, providing employment opportunities for local residents. Increased tourism can also lead to greater exposure and awareness of the site, which can help to promote its preservation and cultural significance.

Tourism can also encourage greater investment in heritage sites. Private investors may be more likely to fund preservation projects if they see potential for a return on their investment through increased tourism. In addition, tourism can attract government funding and support for heritage sites, which can provide additional resources for their preservation and development.

Negative impact of tourism on heritage sites: However, tourism can also have negative impacts on heritage sites. High visitor numbers can lead to overcrowding, damage to the site, and erosion of the site's cultural significance. In addition, tourism can create a "Disneyfication" of heritage sites, with commercialization and entertainment taking precedence over historical accuracy and authenticity. This can lead to a loss of the site's cultural and historical significance, and can create a distorted view of the site's history and cultural significance.

Tourism can also lead to social and environmental impacts. Increased visitor numbers can put pressure on local communities and infrastructure, leading to social and environmental problems such as overcrowding, pollution, and damage to natural resources. Tourism can also lead to displacement of local residents, as land and property prices rise due to tourism demand.

Managing tourism impact on heritage sites: To mitigate the negative impact of tourism on heritage sites, the city can implement various management strategies. These can include visitor management measures such as limiting visitor numbers and restricting access to sensitive areas of the site. The city can also develop educational programs to promote responsible tourism and raise awareness of the cultural and historical significance of the site. In addition, the city can collaborate with local communities and stakeholders to ensure that tourism benefits are shared equitably, and that the site's preservation is prioritized over commercial interests.

Conclusion: Tourism can have both positive and negative impacts on the city's heritage sites. While tourism can bring economic benefits and promote greater awareness of the site, it can also lead to overcrowding, damage to the site, and loss of cultural significance. To manage tourism impact on heritage sites, the city can implement visitor management measures, develop educational programs, and collaborate with local communities and stakeholders to ensure that tourism benefits are shared equitably and that the site's preservation is prioritized over commercial interests.

The city's approach to preserving and promoting its cultural heritage

Preserving a city's cultural heritage is essential to maintain its identity, and promote it to tourists and future generations. In this context, the city has taken several measures to preserve its cultural heritage and promote it to the world.

1. Conservation efforts

Conservation efforts are a key component of preserving a city's cultural heritage. The city has taken various steps to conserve its cultural heritage, such as restoring historic buildings, preserving archaeological sites, and conserving artworks. The city's government has implemented policies to protect and preserve historic buildings, including providing financial support to property owners for restoration works. Many historic buildings have been successfully restored, including several museums, cultural centers, and libraries.

2. Cultural promotion

The city actively promotes its cultural heritage to tourists and locals. The city hosts numerous cultural events throughout the year, such as music and dance performances, art exhibitions, and cultural festivals. These events provide visitors with an opportunity to experience the city's culture and learn about its heritage.

Additionally, the city's government has invested in creating new museums and cultural centers. The city has several well-known museums that showcase the city's history and culture. The museums have extensive collections of artworks, artifacts, and historical objects, and offer guided tours and educational programs.

3. Education

Education is another important aspect of preserving a city's cultural heritage. The city's government has implemented programs to educate residents and visitors about the city's history and culture. Schools in the city teach local history, culture, and language as part of their curriculum. Furthermore, the city has established several cultural centers that offer classes and workshops to teach traditional arts and crafts to the community.

4. Cultural tourism

Tourism plays a vital role in promoting and preserving the city's cultural heritage. The city attracts millions of tourists each year who come to experience the city's unique culture and history. The city has taken several measures to make its cultural heritage more accessible to tourists. For instance, the city has implemented an audio guide system in several museums, which provides visitors with detailed information about the exhibits in various languages.

Additionally, the city offers several heritage tours that take visitors through the city's historic neighborhoods, landmarks, and museums. These tours offer visitors a chance to learn about the city's history and culture from knowledgeable guides.

5. Cultural exchange

Cultural exchange programs are another way the city promotes and preserves its cultural heritage. The city has established partnerships with several cities around the world to exchange cultural experiences. These programs provide an opportunity for artists, performers, and scholars to collaborate and share their knowledge and skills. Additionally, the city has established sister city relationships with several cities worldwide, which helps to promote cultural exchange and tourism.

Conclusion

The city has taken a multi-faceted approach to preserving and promoting its cultural heritage. Through conservation efforts, cultural promotion, education, cultural tourism, and cultural exchange, the city has successfully preserved its rich history and culture for future generations.

The city's cultural heritage is an essential part of its identity and a significant attraction for tourists. By investing in its cultural heritage, the city has established itself as a unique and fascinating destination for visitors from around the world.

Chapter 7: Culture and Society
The city's social and cultural diversity and its impact on the city's identity

The city is often described as a melting pot of different cultures, and this diversity has had a profound impact on the city's identity. This chapter will explore the social and cultural diversity of the city and how it has contributed to the city's cultural identity.

The city is home to people from all over the world, with different ethnicities, religions, and cultural backgrounds. This diversity is reflected in the city's architecture, cuisine, festivals, and celebrations. The city has always been a beacon of hope for people looking for a better life and has welcomed immigrants from all over the world. As a result, the city has become a multicultural hub, with a rich tapestry of cultural influences that have contributed to its unique character.

One of the most visible signs of the city's cultural diversity is its neighborhoods. Each neighborhood has its own distinct character and cultural influences. For example, Little Italy is known for its Italian restaurants and cafes, while Chinatown is home to traditional Chinese shops and markets. The city's African-American neighborhoods are also renowned for their rich cultural heritage, including jazz, blues, and soul music.

The city's cultural diversity is also reflected in its art and entertainment scene. The city has a vibrant arts community, with artists from all over the world showcasing their talents in the city's galleries and museums. The city is also home to world-renowned theaters, such as the Shakespeare Theater, where plays by Shakespeare and other great writers are performed. The city's music scene is equally diverse, with everything from classical and jazz to hip-hop and rock.

The city's cultural diversity is also reflected in its educational institutions. The city has some of the best universities and colleges in the world, attracting students from all over the world. These institutions offer a diverse range of academic programs, from engineering and medicine to the humanities and social sciences. They also provide a platform for students to explore different cultures and perspectives.

Despite its cultural diversity, the city has faced challenges in maintaining social cohesion. Like many other cities around the world, the city has experienced racial tensions and discrimination, particularly in its poorer neighborhoods. However, the city has made efforts to address these issues and promote greater social and cultural integration. For example, the city has implemented policies to encourage greater diversity in its public institutions and has established programs to support marginalized communities.

In conclusion, the city's social and cultural diversity has had a significant impact on its identity. The city's multicultural character has contributed to its unique character and has been reflected in its architecture, cuisine, festivals, and celebrations. While the city has faced challenges in maintaining social cohesion, it has also made significant efforts to promote greater diversity and inclusion. The city's cultural diversity is a source of strength and has played a vital role in shaping the city's cultural identity.

The role of education and media in shaping the city's cultural landscape

Introduction: Education and media play a significant role in shaping a city's cultural landscape by promoting diversity, tolerance, and understanding. In this section, we will explore how education and media have impacted the cultural landscape of our city and what changes have taken place over time.

Education: Education is an essential tool for promoting diversity and tolerance. In our city, education has played a crucial role in shaping the cultural landscape. The city's schools and universities have been at the forefront of promoting cultural diversity and have made significant strides in creating an inclusive learning environment.

One of the city's most notable educational institutions is the University of the City. The university is renowned for its commitment to diversity and has created several programs to promote cultural awareness among its students. These programs include cultural festivals, international student organizations, and language exchange programs.

The city's public schools have also made significant strides in promoting diversity and tolerance. The city's public school system has implemented several programs aimed at promoting cultural awareness among its students. These programs include cultural festivals, multicultural clubs, and language classes.

Media: Media plays a vital role in shaping a city's cultural landscape. In our city, media has played a crucial role in promoting diversity and tolerance. The city has a diverse media landscape, with several newspapers, radio stations, and television networks that cater to different communities.

One of the city's most notable newspapers is The City Times. The newspaper has a diverse staff and covers a wide range of topics that are of interest to the city's diverse communities. The City Times has also been at the forefront of promoting cultural diversity and has created several programs aimed at promoting cultural awareness among its readers.

The city's radio stations and television networks also play a significant role in promoting cultural diversity. The city's radio stations have programs that cater to different communities, such as Spanish-language radio programs, Asian-language radio programs, and African-American radio programs.

Conclusion: In conclusion, education and media play a vital role in shaping a city's cultural landscape. In our city, education and media have been at the forefront of promoting diversity and tolerance. The city's schools and universities have created several programs aimed at promoting cultural awareness among their students, while the city's media landscape caters to different communities and promotes cultural diversity. As the city continues to grow and evolve, education and media will continue to play a significant role in shaping its cultural landscape.

The city's cultural policies and initiatives

The city's cultural policies and initiatives play a vital role in shaping its cultural landscape. In this chapter, we will explore the various policies and initiatives that the city has implemented to promote and preserve its cultural heritage.

One of the most important initiatives that the city has undertaken is the creation of cultural institutions such as museums, art galleries, and cultural centers. These institutions play a critical role in preserving the city's cultural heritage and showcasing its artistic and cultural diversity. They provide a platform for artists and cultural practitioners to showcase their work and promote cultural exchange between different communities.

The city has also implemented various policies to promote cultural diversity and encourage cultural participation among its residents. These policies include initiatives such as funding for cultural events and festivals, grants for artists and cultural practitioners, and support for community-based cultural initiatives.

One of the most significant cultural policies that the city has implemented is the establishment of a cultural district. This district is a designated area of the city that is dedicated to promoting and preserving the city's cultural heritage. It provides a platform for cultural events, festivals, and activities and helps to promote cultural tourism in the city. The district is also home to many cultural institutions, including museums, art galleries, and theaters.

Another important initiative that the city has undertaken is the promotion of cultural education. The city recognizes the importance of cultural education in promoting cultural diversity and understanding, and has implemented various policies and initiatives to promote cultural education in schools and universities. These initiatives include funding for cultural programs and activities in schools, scholarships for students studying the arts and humanities, and support for cultural exchange programs between schools and universities.

The city has also implemented various policies to promote the preservation of its cultural heritage. These policies include initiatives such as the designation of heritage sites and buildings, the protection of historic buildings, and the promotion of traditional crafts and skills.

In recent years, the city has also implemented initiatives to promote cultural sustainability. These initiatives focus on promoting sustainable cultural practices, such as eco-friendly cultural events and festivals, and promoting sustainable tourism practices that prioritize the preservation of cultural heritage.

Overall, the city's cultural policies and initiatives play a critical role in shaping its cultural landscape. They promote cultural diversity and understanding, encourage cultural participation among residents, and promote the preservation of the city's cultural heritage. The city's commitment to promoting and preserving its cultural heritage is a testament to its rich and diverse cultural landscape and its position as a cultural hub in the region.

The challenges and opportunities facing the city's cultural sector

The cultural sector of a city plays a significant role in shaping its identity and character. However, it also faces various challenges that threaten its sustainability and growth. In this subtopic, we will discuss the challenges and opportunities facing the cultural sector of the city and the strategies adopted by the stakeholders to overcome these challenges.

1. Funding and resource constraints: One of the primary challenges faced by the cultural sector is funding and resource constraints. Museums, theaters, galleries, and other cultural institutions require significant investments in infrastructure, staff, and programs. However, funding for the cultural sector is often limited, and resources are stretched thin.

To overcome this challenge, the city's cultural institutions rely on a combination of public and private funding. The government provides grants and subsidies to support cultural programs, while private donors, foundations, and corporations contribute through sponsorships and donations. Additionally, cultural institutions have been exploring innovative revenue streams, such as merchandising, event hosting, and digital content creation.

2. Digitalization and technology: The digitalization of the cultural sector has created both challenges and opportunities. On the one hand, the widespread availability of digital content has increased access to culture and broadened audiences. On the other hand, it has also disrupted traditional revenue models, making it difficult for cultural institutions to monetize their digital content.

To overcome this challenge, cultural institutions are embracing digitalization and technology. Museums and galleries are creating virtual tours and online exhibitions, while theaters and music venues are streaming live performances. Additionally, cultural institutions are using social media and other digital platforms to engage audiences and promote their programs.

3. Demographic shifts: The city's cultural sector is also affected by demographic shifts, such as changing immigration patterns, urbanization, and aging populations. These shifts impact both the supply and demand for cultural programs, as well as the cultural preferences of audiences.

To address this challenge, cultural institutions are adopting inclusive programming that reflects the diversity of the city's population. This includes programming that highlights the cultural traditions of various communities, as well as initiatives that promote cross-cultural exchange and dialogue.

4. Competition and collaboration: The cultural sector faces intense competition from other entertainment options, such as sports, movies, and television. Additionally, cultural institutions must also compete with each other for audiences, funding, and resources. However, there are also opportunities for collaboration between cultural institutions, which can result in shared resources, cross-promotion, and increased visibility.

To overcome this challenge, cultural institutions are collaborating on joint programming and marketing initiatives. Additionally, cultural institutions are exploring partnerships with non-cultural organizations, such as schools, hospitals, and community centers, to expand their reach and impact.

5. Sustainability and resilience: The COVID-19 pandemic has exposed the vulnerability of the cultural sector to external shocks and crises. Cultural institutions have been forced to close their doors, cancel events, and lay off staff. The pandemic has also highlighted the importance of sustainability and resilience in the cultural sector.

To address this challenge, cultural institutions are adopting sustainable business models that prioritize long-term financial stability and resilience. This includes strategies such as diversifying revenue streams, reducing overhead costs, and building emergency reserves.

In conclusion, the challenges and opportunities facing the city's cultural sector are complex and multifaceted. However, by embracing innovation, collaboration, and inclusivity, cultural institutions can overcome these challenges and continue to contribute to the city's cultural landscape and identity.

Conclusion
Summary of the book's main themes and findings

In this concluding chapter, we will summarize the main themes and findings of the book "Exploring the Cultural Identity of [City Name]." Throughout the previous chapters, we have examined various aspects of the city's cultural identity, including literature, language, food, festivals, museums, heritage sites, and society. We have explored how these different elements contribute to the city's cultural identity, and how they have evolved over time.

One of the main themes that emerged from our exploration of the city's cultural identity is diversity. We have seen how the city's social and cultural diversity has shaped its identity, and how this diversity is reflected in its language, food, festivals, and society. We have also seen how the city's cultural policies and initiatives have attempted to embrace and celebrate this diversity, while also promoting social cohesion and inclusion.

Another theme that has emerged is the importance of heritage and tradition. The city's museums and heritage sites play a critical role in preserving its cultural heritage, and many of the city's festivals and celebrations are deeply rooted in tradition and history. However, we have also seen how the city's cultural landscape is constantly evolving, and how new trends and influences are shaping its identity.

Language and literature have also played an important role in shaping the city's cultural identity. We have explored how the city's linguistic diversity has contributed to its unique character, and how its literature reflects the city's history, culture, and values. We have also seen how language and literature can be used as tools for promoting social cohesion and inclusion.

Food and cuisine have emerged as a central component of the city's cultural identity. We have explored the city's culinary traditions and famous dishes, the role of street food and markets, the impact of immigration on the city's cuisine, and the emergence of new food trends. Food has the power to bring people together, to celebrate diversity and tradition, and to create new cultural connections.

Festivals and celebrations are another key component of the city's cultural identity. We have examined the city's major festivals and celebrations and their historical and cultural significance, the role of religion and spirituality in these events, the evolution of the city's festival culture over time, and the impact of festivals on the city's cultural identity. Festivals and celebrations are important markers of the city's cultural identity, and they play a critical role in promoting social cohesion and inclusivity.

Finally, we have explored the role of museums and heritage sites in preserving the city's cultural heritage, the impact of tourism on these sites, and the city's approach to preserving and promoting its cultural heritage. Museums and heritage sites are critical to preserving the city's history and culture, and they also serve as important educational and cultural resources for residents and visitors alike.

In conclusion, "Exploring the Cultural Identity of [City Name]" has provided a comprehensive examination of the city's cultural identity, examining various aspects of its history, culture, language, food, festivals, museums, heritage sites, and society. Through this exploration, we have seen how the city's diversity, heritage, and traditions, as well as its evolving cultural landscape, contribute to its unique character and identity. The city's cultural policies and initiatives play an important role in promoting social cohesion and inclusivity, while also celebrating its rich cultural heritage and embracing new cultural influences.

As the book draws to a close, it is worth reflecting on the importance of history and culture in shaping a city's identity. Cities are more than just collections of buildings and infrastructure; they are living, breathing entities with their own unique personalities and identities. And much of what makes a city distinctive and memorable comes from its history and cultural heritage.

Throughout this book, we have explored various aspects of history and culture in the context of a particular city. We have seen how the city's geography, economy, and demographics have shaped its culture and how its culture, in turn, has helped to define its identity. We have looked at how the city's architecture, food, festivals, museums, and social diversity all contribute to its unique character. And we have seen how the city's cultural policies and initiatives can help to preserve and promote its heritage.

One of the key themes that emerges from this exploration is the idea that history and culture are deeply intertwined. The stories we tell about a city's past help to shape our understanding of its present and our vision for its future. They give us a sense of continuity and connection to the past, while also providing us with a foundation for building a better future.

Another important theme is the idea that culture is a constantly evolving and dynamic entity. A city's culture is never static; it is always changing and adapting to new circumstances and influences. This is particularly true in today's globalized world, where cities are increasingly interconnected and influenced by one another. As a result, it is more important than ever to embrace cultural diversity and celebrate the many different voices and perspectives that make a city unique.

At the same time, however, it is important to recognize the challenges and threats that can arise when a city's cultural identity is under pressure. Rapid urbanization, globalization, and economic development can all put a strain on a city's cultural heritage, leading to the loss of historic buildings, traditions, and ways of life. This is why it is so important for cities to have strong cultural policies and initiatives in place to help preserve and promote their heritage.

In conclusion, this book has demonstrated the vital role that history and culture play in shaping a city's identity. It has shown how a city's cultural heritage can be a source of pride and inspiration, as well as a foundation for building a better future. And it has highlighted the many challenges and opportunities that arise when a city's cultural identity is under pressure. By embracing cultural diversity, promoting cultural preservation, and celebrating the many unique aspects of our cities, we can ensure that they continue to thrive and evolve for generations to come.

Implications for the city's future cultural development

As we have explored throughout this book, a city's culture and heritage play a vital role in shaping its identity and defining its place in the world. It is clear that the cultural landscape of a city is constantly evolving, and it is important for cities to take an active role in preserving and promoting their cultural heritage while also embracing new forms of cultural expression. In this final chapter, we will discuss the implications of our findings for the future cultural development of the city.

First and foremost, it is important for the city to continue to prioritize cultural preservation and promotion. This means investing in the maintenance and restoration of historic buildings, monuments, and museums, as well as creating new initiatives to celebrate the city's cultural heritage. For example, the city could host more cultural festivals, events, and exhibitions to showcase its diversity and history. These initiatives would not only benefit the city's cultural sector but also provide opportunities for economic growth through tourism and cultural exchange.

Furthermore, the city must recognize the importance of supporting and nurturing its creative industries. This includes supporting local artists, musicians, writers, and designers, as well as investing in cultural education and programs that cultivate creativity and innovation. By doing so, the city can ensure that it remains at the forefront of cultural expression and development.

Another important aspect of the city's cultural development is the need to address social and cultural inequalities. The city must take steps to ensure that all members of its community have access to cultural opportunities and that diverse perspectives and voices are represented in the cultural landscape. This includes supporting and celebrating the contributions of marginalized communities, as well as creating opportunities for cultural exchange and dialogue.

Finally, the city must be open to new forms of cultural expression and development. This means embracing emerging trends and technologies while also respecting and preserving traditional cultural practices. The city should foster a climate of creativity and experimentation that encourages cultural innovation and growth.

In conclusion, our exploration of the city's history, culture, and identity has demonstrated the crucial role that these elements play in shaping the city's future. By investing in cultural preservation and promotion, supporting the creative industries, addressing social and cultural inequalities, and embracing new forms of cultural expression and development, the city can ensure that it remains a vibrant and dynamic cultural center for generations to come.

THE END

To help you better understand the language and concepts related to aging and older adults, below you will find a list of key terms and their definitions.

1. Cultural Identity: The collective identity of a group of people, formed by the shared values, traditions, beliefs, customs, and practices that define their way of life.

2. City: A large and densely populated urban area, characterized by diverse social, cultural, and economic activities.

3. History: The study of past events, particularly those relating to a particular place or people, and their significance in shaping the present.

4. Heritage: The tangible and intangible aspects of a society's cultural inheritance, including buildings, monuments, artifacts, customs, and traditions.

5. Contemporary Society: The present-day society and its cultural norms, values, and practices.

6. Cultural Diversity: The existence of multiple cultural groups within a society, characterized by differences in language, religion, ethnicity, and customs.

7. Tradition: The customs and beliefs that are handed down from generation to generation and form an integral part of a society's cultural identity.

8. Preservation: The act of protecting and maintaining cultural heritage for future generations.

9. Identity Formation: The process by which individuals and groups construct and negotiate their sense of identity through social interactions, cultural practices, and historical events.

10. Cultural Policy: The government's strategies and initiatives aimed at promoting and preserving cultural diversity and heritage.

Supporting Materials

Introduction:

- Florida, R. (2002). The rise of the creative class. Basic Books.

- Landry, C. (2008). The creative city: A toolkit for urban innovators. Earthscan.

Chapter 1: Architecture and Landmarks

- Frampton, K. (1992). Modern architecture: A critical history (3rd ed.). Thames and Hudson.

- Pile, J. (2005). A history of interior design (2nd ed.). Laurence King Publishing.

Chapter 2: Arts and Entertainment

- Bianchini, F., & Parkinson, M. (Eds.). (1993). Cultural policy and urban regeneration: The west European experience. Manchester University Press.

- Florida, R. (2012). The rise of the creative class--revisited: 10th anniversary edition. Basic Books.

Chapter 3: Literature and Language

- Eagleton, T. (2008). Literary theory: An introduction (3rd ed.). Wiley-Blackwell.

- Fishman, J. A. (Ed.). (2001). Can threatened languages be saved? Reversing language shift, revisited: A 21st century perspective (Vol. 90). Multilingual Matters.

Chapter 4: Food and Cuisine

- Albala, K. (2011). Food cultures of the world encyclopedia. ABC-CLIO.
- Counihan, C. M., & Van Esterik, P. (Eds.). (2013). Food and culture: A reader. Routledge.
Chapter 5: Festivals and Celebrations
- Smith, V. L. (1995). Hosts and guests revisited: Tourism issues of the 21st century. Cognizant Communication Corporation.
- Urry, J. (1995). Consuming places. Routledge.
Chapter 6: Museums and Heritage Sites
- Hooper-Greenhill, E. (Ed.). (2000). Museums and the interpretation of visual culture. Routledge.
- Kavanagh, G. (1996). Making histories in museums. Leicester University Press.
Chapter 7: Culture and Society
- Castells, M. (1996). The rise of the network society (Vol. 1). John Wiley & Sons.
- Zukin, S. (1995). The cultures of cities. Blackwell Publishers.
Conclusion:
- Harvey, D. (2012). Rebel cities: From the right to the city to the urban revolution. Verso.
- UNESCO. (1982). Mexico city declaration on cultural policies. Retrieved from http://portal.unesco.org/en/ev.php-

URL_ID=13178&URL_DO=DO_TOPIC&URL_SECTION=2
01.html